I0796282

Agriculture
MICHELLE LOMBERG
LIGHTBOX
openlightbox.com

Lightbox is an all-inclusive digital solution for the teaching and learning of curriculum topics in an original, groundbreaking way. Lightbox is based on National Curriculum Standards.

STANDARD FEATURES OF LIGHTBOX

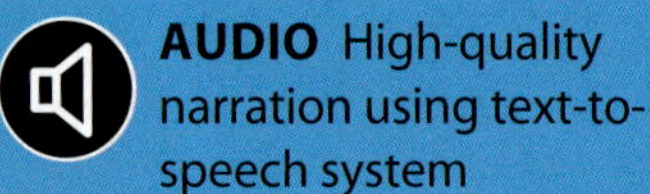

AUDIO High-quality narration using text-to-speech system

ACTIVITIES Printable PDFs that can be emailed and graded

SLIDESHOWS Pictorial overviews of key concepts

VIDEOS Embedded high-definition video clips

WEBLINKS Curated links to external, child-safe resources

TRANSPARENCIES Step-by-step layering of maps, diagrams, charts, and timelines

INTERACTIVE MAPS Interactive maps and aerial satellite imagery

QUIZZES Ten multiple choice questions that are automatically graded and emailed for teacher assessment

KEY WORDS Matching key concepts to their definitions

CONTENTS

Agriculture in the United States

Most people know that the foods they eat are products of agriculture. However, clothes, shoes, and even motor fuel can all be agricultural products, too. Cotton, wool, linen, and leather are all products of agriculture. So are biofuels.

BANANAS are the **number one fruit crop** in the world.

40% of the global population works in the **agricultural industry.**

1 ACRE of **soybeans** produces **82,368 crayons.** (0.4 hectares)

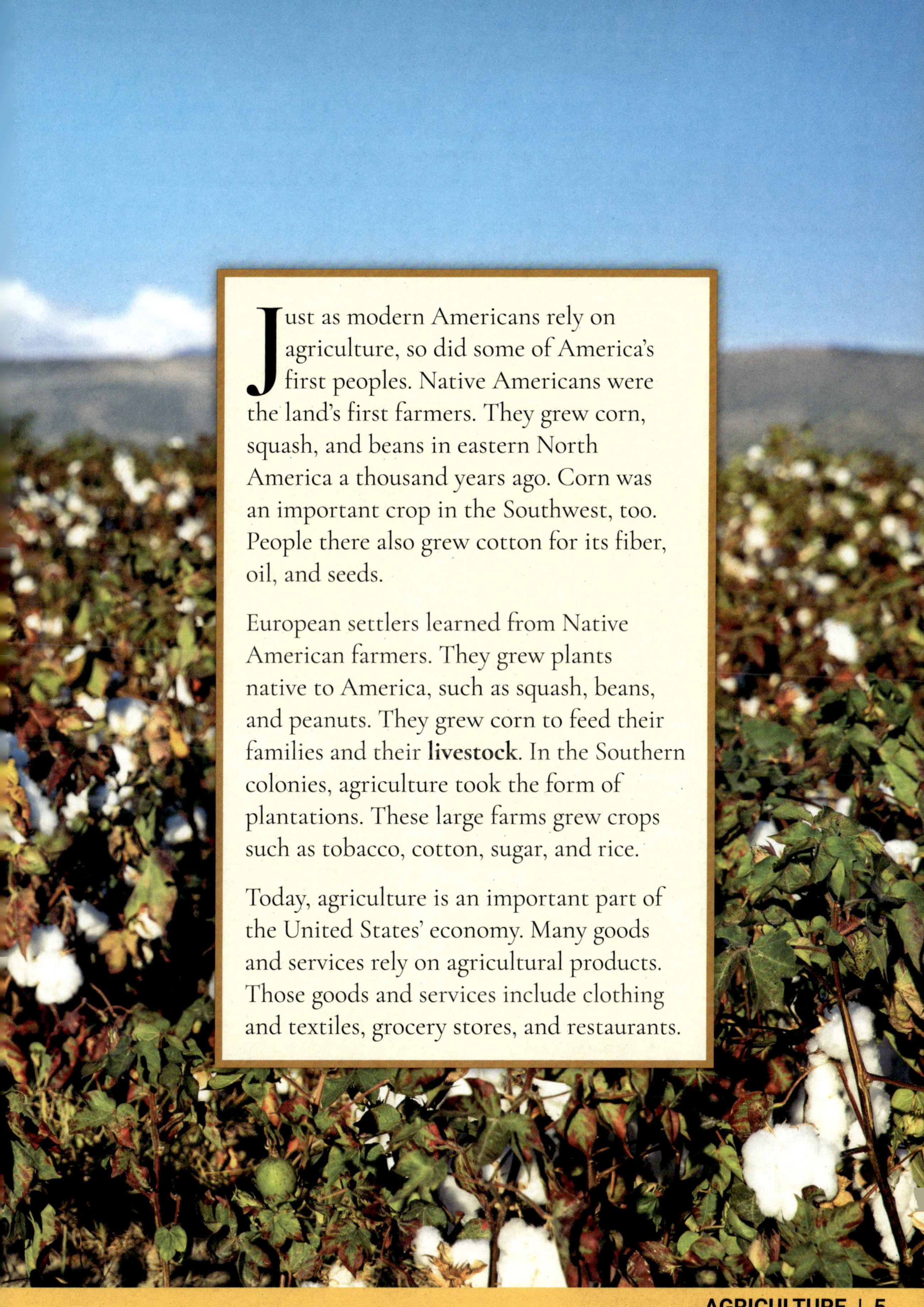

Just as modern Americans rely on agriculture, so did some of America's first peoples. Native Americans were the land's first farmers. They grew corn, squash, and beans in eastern North America a thousand years ago. Corn was an important crop in the Southwest, too. People there also grew cotton for its fiber, oil, and seeds.

European settlers learned from Native American farmers. They grew plants native to America, such as squash, beans, and peanuts. They grew corn to feed their families and their **livestock**. In the Southern colonies, agriculture took the form of plantations. These large farms grew crops such as tobacco, cotton, sugar, and rice.

Today, agriculture is an important part of the United States' economy. Many goods and services rely on agricultural products. Those goods and services include clothing and textiles, grocery stores, and restaurants.

Agriculture Then and Now

Farmers and ranchers have always worked hard, but **innovations** in agriculture over the past two centuries have made farm work easier. The industrial revolution reached America in the late 1700s. Industrialization brought important changes to farming.

Plowing the Field

Farmers use plows to loosen soil before planting seeds. In the past, oxen or horses pulled a plow through the field. Today, plows are pulled behind tractors or other farm machines.

THEN

NOW

Harvesting the Grain

Cutting crops and separating the grains was done by hand before horse-drawn cutters appeared in the 1800s. Today, a combine cuts the stalks and separates the grains at the same time.

NOW

The invention of machines such as mechanical **reapers**, planters, and cutters meant that it was easier to grow and harvest more crops. Inventions such as poultry incubators and cream separators increased the amount of products such as eggs and milk that farms could produce. These changes left farmers with surplus products to sell.

In the late 1800s, the American population increased rapidly as immigrants arrived from all over the world. There was a huge demand for food. Today, there are far more Americans than there were then. Computer-assisted machines and even robots have replaced the hand tools and animals used in the past, so farmers can produce even more crops, meat, and other products.

Milking the Cows

People milked cows by hand before 1865, when the first milking machine was invented. Today, robotic machines milk cows in huge automated parlors with almost no human involvement.

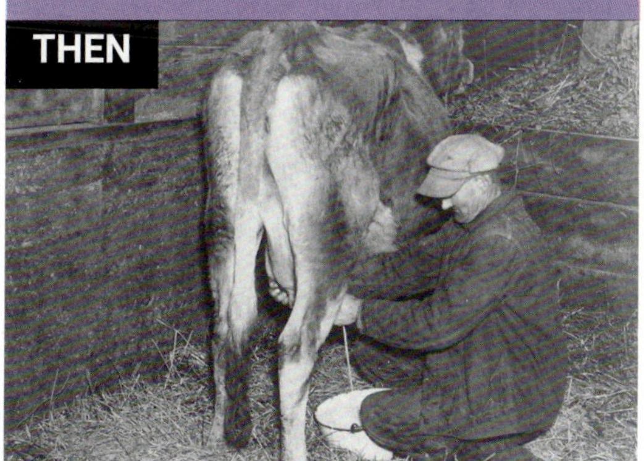

Taking Cattle to Market

Western movies often feature cowboys on horseback driving a herd of cattle into town. Today, cattle still need to be rounded up, but they are driven to the **market** in semi-trailer trucks.

Farmland in the United States

If all the farms in the country were laid out next to one another, they would cover an area twice the size of Mexico. Farmland occupies some 915 million acres (370.3 million hectares) in the United States. The crops farmers grow and the livestock they raise depend on the climate and soil type of the region where they live.

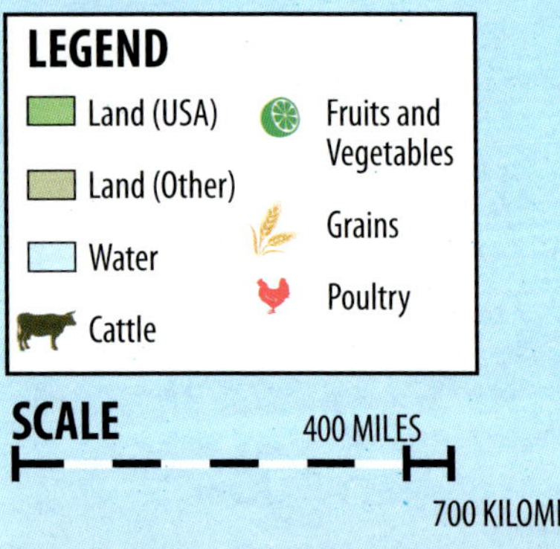

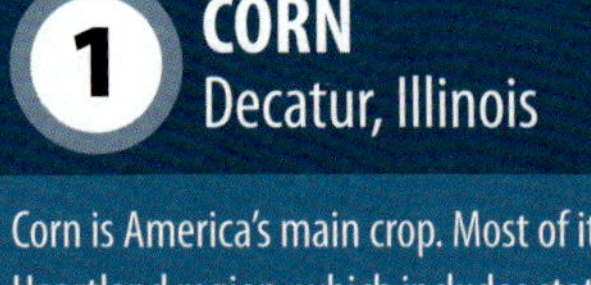

1 CORN
Decatur, Illinois

Corn is America's main crop. Most of it is grown in the Heartland region, which includes states such as Illinois, Iowa, and Indiana. Decatur, Illinois, is home to world's largest corn wet mill. Wet milling is used to turn corn into a wide range of products, including corn oil.

2 CATTLE
Kingsville, Texas

It makes sense that longhorn cattle are a symbol of Texas. The state is the top producer of cattle and calves. Texan farmers raise 11.7 million of the country's 92 million cattle and calves. The King Ranch near Kingsville Texas has some 35,000 cattle and is one of the largest ranches in the world.

3 FRUIT
San Joaquin Valley, California

California farms and orchards make up 80 percent of the land in the United States devoted to fruit, tree nut, and berry production. The San Joaquin Valley is home to Sun Pacific, the largest kiwifruit grower in the United States. California produces 99 percent of U.S. kiwifruit, and most of the rest of the country's fruit and vegetables.

4 POULTRY
Springdale, Arkansas

Arkansas is among the top 10 producers of **broiler chickens**, turkeys, and eggs. Poultry is big business in Arkansas, where it employs more than 40,000 people. Poultry accounts for 40 percent of the state's income from livestock. Springdale is home to Tyson Foods, biggest producer of chickens in the U.S.

Agricultural Products Ranked by Importance

Agriculture contributes more than $177 billion to the U.S. economy each year. That is about 1 percent of the country's **gross domestic product (GDP)**. When industries related to agriculture are added, including food and beverage sales and service, textiles, clothing, and leather products, the total is more than $985 billion. That is 5.7 percent of the national GDP.

Fields of golden wheat cover thousands of square miles (square kilometers) in some regions of the United States.

Cattle and calves lead sales of U.S. agricultural products. Texas, Nebraska, and Kansas are the top producers of beef cattle. Wisconsin, California, and New York produce the most dairy cattle. These dairy cows produce the country's third highest-selling agricultural product, which is milk and dairy goods. Dairy products include fresh, canned, and dry milk, together with cheese, butter, ice cream and other frozen foods, plus yogurt and whey.

ONE QUARTER of all meat consumed in the United States comes from **HOGS**.

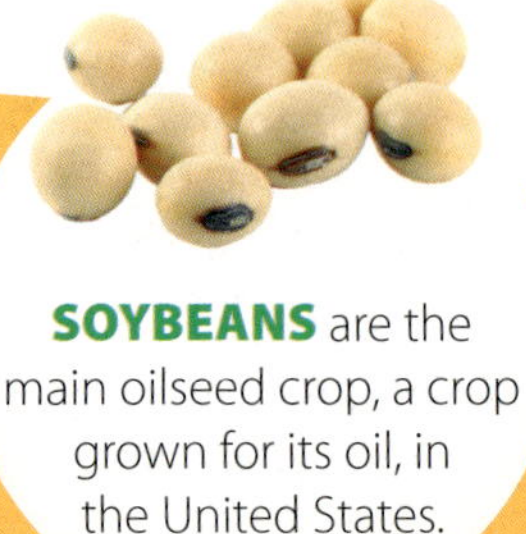

SOYBEANS are the main oilseed crop, a crop grown for its oil, in the United States.

Top 10 U.S. Agricultural Product Sales in 2015

$78 BILLION	Cattle and Calves
$47 BILLION	Corn
$36 BILLION	Milk and Dairy Products
$33 BILLION	Soybeans
$29 BILLION	Broiler Chickens
$21 BILLION	Hogs
$19 BILLION	Miscellaneous Crops
$13 BILLION	Chicken Eggs
$9 BILLION	Wheat
$7 BILLION	Hay

Corn is the country's most valuable crop, and the second-most valuable agricultural product overall. Iowa, Illinois, Minnesota, and Nebraska lead the country in corn sales. More than half of all sales of corn come from these four states. This region of the Midwest is sometimes called the Corn Belt.

Farmers grow corn to provide sweet corn, but also as fodder to feed their animals. Corn makes up 95 percent of feed grain production.

Timeline of Agricultural Events

Over four centuries, agriculture has changed greatly. New farming methods and inventions have improved farming. However, natural disasters have also had a negative impact.

1600 | 1700 | 1750 | 1800 | 1850

1614. Tobacco, the first American agricultural **export**, is shipped from Jamestown Colony, Virginia.

1785. The Philadelphia Society for Promoting Agriculture is founded.

1834. Cyrus McCormick patents the first mechanical reaper.

1932 to 1936. Drought and dust storms cause severe damage to farms in North America.

2015. The Federal Aviation Administration changes its laws to allow farmers to use **drones** to monitor the health of their crops.

1900 | 1950 | 2000 | 2010 | THE FUTURE

Future. Drones will use precise computer programs to figure out the best use of water and **fertilizer** to maximize crops.

2008. The Food and Drug Administration approves the meat and milk of **cloned** animals for consumption.

U.S. Agriculture in the World

America's first farmers grew crops and raised animals, in order to feed and clothe themselves and their families. Today, agriculture is a global enterprise. The United States both exports and **imports** agricultural products worth billions of dollars.

The United States supplies about 4 percent of the world's tomato exports, making it the seventh largest tomato producer.

U.S. farmers and ranchers are among the most productive in the world. The United States ranks third in world food production, after China and India. It is the top producer of corn and soybeans in the world, and is the world's third-ranking producer of wheat. The United States is also the world's top producer of beef.

Cereal grains and livestock products have been the top U.S. farm exports since the late 1800s. Today, however, horticultural products are overtaking these categories. Horticultural products include a broad range of goods, such as fruit, vegetables, nuts, herbs, spices, cut flowers, house plants, and garden plants.

HALF of the fresh fruit and fruit juice Americans enjoy comes from **ABROAD.**

The United States is the world's **fifth-largest** producer of **HONEY.**

The United States leads the world in agricultural exports, and U.S. farmers sell their products to consumers all over the world. About one-fifth of U.S. agricultural products are sold abroad, including more than half of U.S. wheat and rice, and more than 70 percent of U.S. cotton and tree nuts. In 2015, these exports amounted to more than $130 billion. The United States ranks first in the world in exports of corn, soybeans, and wheat. The country is the world's second-largest exporter of broiler chickens.

Canada is the top buyer of U.S. agricultural products. It is followed by China and Mexico. However, Japan is the number-one destination for U.S. beef and corn.

The United States imports agricultural products, too. Canada and Mexico supply most of these imports, which are mostly meat, snack foods, and horticultural products. Horticultural products make up the bulk of agricultural imports, followed by sugar and tropical products such as rubber, cocoa, and coffee.

U.S. farmers raise nearly 9 billion broiler chickens every year. About 16 percent of these broiler chickens are exported.

Facing the Issues

Americans benefit from agriculture in many ways. The industry provides jobs and money for the whole country. Agriculture provides foods, as well as materials for other products, such as textiles, cosmetics, and medicines. Many of these benefits, however, come at an environmental cost.

Some farming practices cause environmental damage, such as soil **erosion** and water **contamination**. Erosion by wind and water removes fertile **topsoil** from fields, which makes the fields less productive. Some farmers use herbicides and pesticides to kill weeds and harmful insects. These chemicals, along with fertilizers and manure, can be carried into surface and **groundwater**. As a result, sources of drinking water can become polluted.

Long revolving booms drip water onto pieces of land so that farmers can grow crops even in naturally dry parts of the country.

Debate

Many farmers in drought-prone regions rely on **irrigation** systems. These systems draw water from the same surface or underground sources that supply water to homes and businesses. Should state governments pass laws to limit agricultural water use?

YES

- Irrigation is depleting underground water supplies.
- The agricultural industry's economic benefit is too small to justify its water use. For example, in California, agriculture accounts for 80 percent of all water use, but contributes only 1.5 percent of the state's GDP.
- Some heavily irrigated crops are exported and do not benefit local people.

NO

- Limiting farmers' water use may endanger the food supply.
- Exports of farm products bring money into the economy.
- New irrigation technologies, such as drip irrigation systems that send water directly to plants' roots, can help farmers use water more efficiently.

Hydroponic plants grow with their roots in water rather than soil.

Looking to the Future

In the past 60 years, the **productivity** of U.S. farms has more than doubled. This is due to advances in science and technology that have improved agricultural chemicals and machinery. Science and technology will continue to play a role in keeping agriculture productive and sustainable in the future.

Farmers increasingly use **genetic engineering** to improve crops and livestock. Genetic engineering has created plants that are resistant to pests and dairy cows that are resistant to **udder** infections. In the future, cloning farm animals may become common. Cloning allows farmers to create genetic copies of their best livestock.

New farm-equipment technology allows farmers to use the **Global Positioning System (GPS)** to steer farm machines in fog or darkness. Farmers can also use GPS-based mobile apps to map fields, sample soil, and monitor crops. In the near future, innovations will likely include the use of drones and self-driving machines. These machines will allow farmers to apply fertilizers, pesticides, herbicides, and water precisely where they are needed. This will reduce waste and decrease the possibility of contaminating the soil or water supplies.

Drones will enable farmers to monitor their crops. They carry cameras that reveal whether or not plants are growing healthily.

Careers in Agriculture

A career in agriculture is a good choice for people who like fresh air and animals. Those who enjoy teamwork and problem solving, experimenting in a lab, or tinkering in a machine shop can also earn a living in agriculture and agricultural fields. About 10 percent of workers in the United States are employed in agriculture and related industries.

Ranch Manager
Ranch managers make sure work gets done on the farm. They supervise other workers and assign daily tasks. Ranch managers are also responsible for livestock. They plan breeding programs and keep detailed records of all animals born on the ranch or shipped from it.

Duties: Managing the daily operations of a livestock farm

Education: **Apprenticeship** training or college certificate in agriculture

Interests: Animals, record keeping, and accounting

Soil and Plant Scientist
Soil and plant scientists study how plants interact with soil. They often work with farmers to help achieve high yields. Their work usually involves collecting soil samples and soil data. Soil scientists work for government agencies and private companies, or at universities.

Duties: Analyzing soil samples to improve crop yields

Education: Bachelor's degree in soil science

Interests: **Botany**, chemistry, **hydrology**, and geology

Farm Equipment Mechanic
Farm equipment mechanics repair and service the machinery used on farms. Some work for farm equipment dealers, while others are self-employed. They do most of their work in a shop, but they may be called onto the field to make emergency repairs.

Duties: Repairing machinery such as tractors, harvesters, milking machines, and irrigation systems

Education: Training in heavy-equipment repair at a vocational school, as well as on-the-job training

Interests: Problem solving and physical work

Activity

Three Sisters Research Project

The Iroquois people of eastern North America grew corn, squash, and beans together. They called these plants the Three Sisters.

The three plants help each other grow. The cornstalk gives the bean a structure to climb. At the same time, the bean enriches the soil with **nitrogen**, which helps provide nutrition for the other plants. The squash keeps the ground moist and stops weeds from growing. This helps the corn to grow.

Research the Three Sisters legend. You will need these items:

- Notebook or paper
- Pen or pencil to record findings
- Colored pencils or paints
- Access to your school library or internet

Instructions

1. Use your school library or the internet to research the Native American legend of the three sisters. Try to find multiple Iroquois versions of the story. Note the differences between them.
2. Retell the legend in your own words.
3. Use colored pencils of paints to illustrate your story. Look up Iroquois styles of art in books or on the internet. Use them to create illustrations in a similar style or choose another style you prefer.
4. Think about the different versions of the story. How much did they differ? In what ways were they similar? Why do you think this might be the case?

Quiz

Check out how much you have learned about agriculture in the United States. The answers to all these questions are in this book.

ONE
Which farm animal is a symbol of Texas?

TWO
What animal provides a quarter of all meat eaten in the United States?

THREE
Most fruit farming in the United States takes place in which state?

FOUR
More than half of all sales of corn come from which four states?

FIVE
What do farmers use to kill harmful insects on plants?

SIX
What did Cyrus McCormick invent?

SEVEN
What are the world's top three food-producing countries?

EIGHT
What are soybeans used for?

NINE
What are two examples of environmental damage that farming can cause?

TEN
What is America's main crop?

ANSWERS

ONE Longhorn cattle **TWO** Hogs **THREE** California
FOUR Iowa, Illinois, Minnesota, and Nebraska
FIVE Insecticides **SIX** Mechanical reaper **SEVEN** China, India, and the United States **EIGHT** As an oilseed crop
NINE Soil erosion and water contamination **TEN** Corn

Key Words

agriculture: farming

apprenticeship: a period of on-the-job training

botany: the study of plants

broiler chickens: chickens raised for their meat

cereal grains: the edible seeds of plants such as wheat, corn, barley, oats, and rice

cloned: created in a laboratory using genetic material from one parent

contamination: pollution

drones: remote-controlled flying craft

drought: an extended period of dry weather

erosion: wearing or washing away

export: sell to buyers in other countries

fertilizer: chemicals or matter added to soil to help plants grow

genetic engineering: a practice that allows scientists to alter the genes of a plant or animal in order to introduce improvements

global positioning system (GPS): the system of satellites and receivers that allows users to precisely locate sites on Earth

gross domestic product (GDP): the dollar value of all goods and services produced in a given time and place

hydrology: the study of the properties of water on and below Earth's surface and in the atmosphere

imports: buys goods from other countries

innovations: new ideas, objects, or ways of doing things

irrigation: artificial watering

livestock: animals raised on farms

market: a place where products can be bought or sold

nitrogen: a chemical element that plants absorb as a nutrient from the soil

productivity: the measure of how much a farm produces, compared to the labor and resources used

reapers: machines that cut down plants

topsoil: surface soil in which plants grow

udder: the milk-producing organ in cows

Index

LIGHTBOX

SUPPLEMENTARY RESOURCES

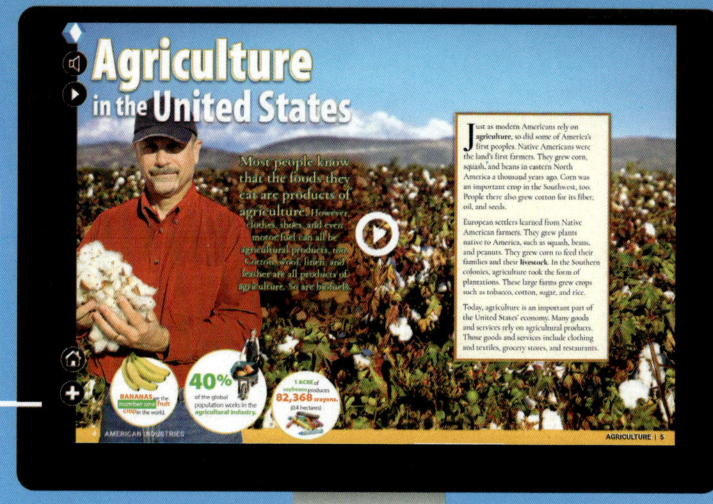

Click on the plus icon found in the bottom left corner of each spread to open additional teacher resources.

- Download and print the book's quizzes and activities
- Access curriculum correlations
- Explore additional web applications that enhance the Lightbox experience

LIGHTBOX DIGITAL TITLES

Packed full of integrated media

VIDEOS

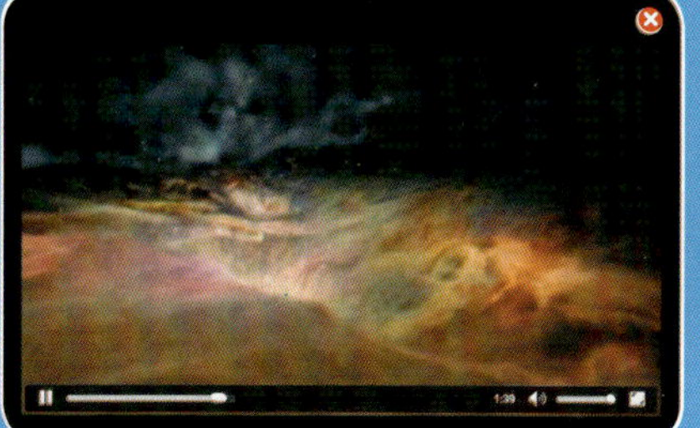

INTERACTIVE MAPS

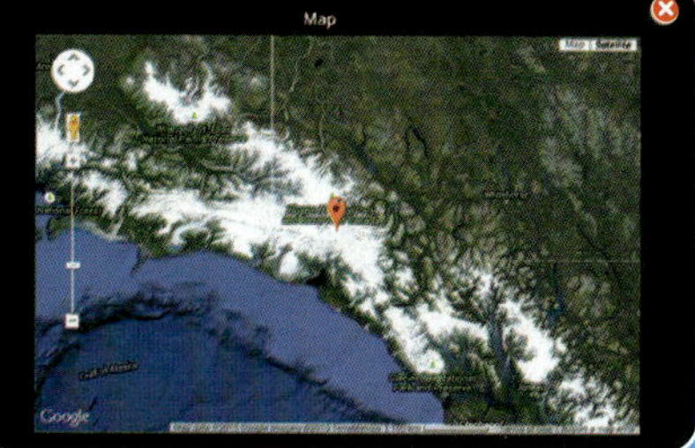

WEBLINKS

SLIDESHOWS

QUIZZES

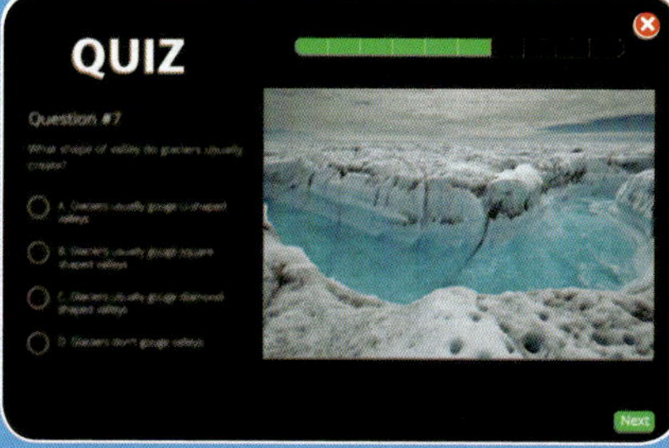

OPTIMIZED FOR

✓ TABLETS
✓ WHITEBOARDS
✓ COMPUTERS
✓ AND MUCH MORE!

Published by Smartbook Media Inc.
350 5th Avenue, 59th Floor New York, NY 10118
Website: www.openlightbox.com

Library of Congress Cataloging-in-Publication Data
Names: Lomberg, Michelle, author.
Title: Agriculture / Michelle Lomberg.
Other titles: American industries (Smartbook Media Inc.)
Description: New York, NY : Smartbook Media Inc., 2018. | Series: American industries | Includes index.
Identifiers: LCCN 2016056287 (print) | LCCN 2016059190 (ebook) | ISBN 9781510519299 (hard cover : alk. paper) | ISBN 9781510519305 (multi-user ebk.)
Subjects: LCSH: Agriculture--United States--Juvenile literature.
Classification: LCC S519 .L66 2018 (print) | LCC S519 (ebook) | DDC 338.10973--dc23
LC record available at https://lccn.loc.gov/2016056287

Printed in the United States of America in Brainerd, Minnesota
1 2 3 4 5 6 7 8 9 0 21 20 19 18 17

062017
032217

Editor: Katie Gillespie
Art Director: Terry Paulhus

Every reasonable effort has been made to trace ownership and to obtain permission to reprint copyright material. The publisher would be pleased to have any errors or omissions brought to its attention so that they may be corrected in subsequent printings. The publisher acknowledges Getty Images, iStock, Shutterstock, Thinkstock, Dreamstime, Alamy, Library of Congress, and Newscom as its primary image suppliers for this title.